T0161219

The Lowly Negro

James Smith

REVOLUTIONARY BOOKS
publishing

Acknowledgments

I want to give a special thanks to the park bench philosophers, street corner prophets, prostitutes, drug dealers, conscious poets, emcees, filmmakers, ex-wives, lovers, haters, family, friends (real and fake) and my enemies who assisted me in becoming a man.

Credits

© 2022 James Smith
Library of Congress Control Number: 2021932882
ISBN: 978-0-578-86097-8
Printed in China
All Rights Reserved

ATTENTION: SCHOOLS, PRISONS, CAFES, JUVENILLE DETENTION CENTERS, MENTAL HEALTH HOSPITALS, LIBRARIES AND ANY AND ALL BUSINESSES.

Revolutionary Books are available at quantity discounts with bulk purchase for educational, business or sales promotional use.

Email: publisher@revolutionarybookspublishing.com

Contact

View my life and work: Instagram @jamessmithpoet
Write to me: jamessmithpoet@gmail.com

Thank you for reading this book.

Dedicated to my son Lucien,
my daughter Maya

"The most dangerous creation of any society is the man who has nothing to lose."

— James Baldwin

WITHERING AWAY TO NOTHINGNESS

How many men cut down by expectation

Residue of ambition, a barrage of
self-doubt

Resistance surrenders unresponsive
for the betterment of transparent
clarity

What has man accomplished and who has
benefited

In his last breath what would the
narcissistic dreamer say; I wish I
made better choices, I wish I had
another chance

What wishes does this foolhardy man
regurgitate

Station as prey: poor, ignorant,
young, weak

Existing check to check one sickness
away from defeat

Fragmented version of self, withering
away to nothingness

ABOVE THE TIDE

Candlelight flickers into night
The unwieldy sweltering sky
Thoughts keep my head above the tide
Nature's innocents have taken flight
Hundreds of years ripped from earth
Candlelight flickers into night
Weight of water exudes flesh
Insects feast on forboded nectar
Thoughts keep my head above the tide
Hummingbirds fly roaring with light
God's breath on their wings to sustain
Candlelight flickers into night
Victim becomes perpetrator
Extremity of reason to survive
Candlelight flickers into night
Thoughts keep my head above the tide

THE RUNNER

Becoming familiar with denial,

trepidation increases the swell

Running on empty at the height

of the season

AUDACITY OF YOUTH

Audacity of youth induced to ruins

Disillusionment circumvents false

positives

Vile malignant narcissist in turmoil

FOG OF WAR

Surrender concedes

Rhetoric transparent

Lies resonate truths

Victims await you

Death collects his due

GOD EATS DOG

God's alter ego is the Devil

In God's likeness, God and Man

equal parts good and evil

L(I)KE

Do I like YOU
At first glimpse reality is escapism
Stylized theatre on IG
Transient stages appear, re-appear and disappear
What remains is the real YOU
Characterized narcissistic sociopath
Influencers and celebrities mirroring vanity
Peripheral: entitled, apathetic, sensitive,
selfish
At your moment of dissension who will favor YOU
Descending fame and infamy: a younger, hipper,
slimmer, prettier YOU
Your last words: If only I stood for something
greater than myself
If only I
There is no I in US and YOU never cared about US
YOU only cared about YOU and I was the solitary
I in L(I)KE
I'll soon forget YOU with one flick of my thumb
Wasted life squandered with meaningless
superficial posts
L(I)FE lived without passion, conviction and
purpose
Do I like YOU

TWO BEASTS

Perched between two beasts
as if we're old acquaintances
Never any faces familiar in here
Can't stop thinking, I'm trapped

THE BAR IS CLOSING

Last dance, the bar is closing

Water's up to her neck, how much longer

can she hold on

Afraid to fall asleep, she doesn't know

where she'll wake

Lived a simple life, listening to

Satchmo, sipping on air

Falling, drifting under lucid spell

She can't go any further; her will to

survive diminishing

One day she'll forgive, wishing it

could go back to the way it was

OLD MAN

Old man told me today,

getting old is the hardest deed

he ever had to do

THE HARD TRUTHS

Conditioned by Religion,
Politicians, and Madison Avenue
Disillusioned, old, and forgotten
envying the arrogance of youth
Idealists instinctively reach for
stars falling short of the mark
Savage and barbarous minus the sum
of humanity
Importance of survival a deliberate
farce
Human embodiment and residual of
shame

THE RABBIT & THE DOWNWARD SPIRAL

The struggle 'to be' is the driving force behind his existence. To aim for the highest attainable star in the universe and at any cost secure the position. His life filled with sadness of truth that exhibits before him in all its fashion. And when he looks back 30 years down the line in all honesty, what will he see? An older rapidly aging version of himself on his birthday that seems to arrive 4 times a year. In his veins the evidence of a life polluted with the strains of decadence and self-medication. Decrepit, neglected and invisible, his reward as he closes his eyes to reminisce about past distinction in a kinder forgiving light. Inflicted with aches and pains pulsating through arteries and veins to the end roads of this man's life. Who is this demon lurking beneath the realms of senses? Persuading whims and desires to sacrifice all that is good and real for vanity and superficiality.

Or is it? Is he, his own enemy? Could he
be the saboteur of his demise? Failure his
destiny, his fate, his fault. Worked hard to
make all the right connections. We are
not one of you and you are not one of us.
The man woke, realized he was on the wrong
side of the street. How did he not see the signs?
Someone or something must be to blame.
Perhaps he went back to sleep after he shut off
the alarm.

"The Negro has been here in America since 1619…He is not going anywhere else; this country is his home. He wants to do his part to help make this city, state, and nation a better place for everyone regardless of color and race."

— Medgar Evers

THE LOWLY NEGRO

Beware the bearer who provokes envy

Words become numbers, volumes muted

Consumerism his fetish: the prey,

my brethren, the lowly Negro

Eyes toward the ground

Devil intuitively watches

Bearer who sets the trap

Malicious and mischievous coward

Convinced the World he means no harm

DIXIELAND

Dixieland, I despise you

In exile, trapped in your polluted womb

Surrounded by insolent rednecks,

dull-witted and sadistic by nature

Counting the days until I AM FREE

NIGGERPHOBIA

Am I a Nigger

What is the Nigger's purpose

Fondling master's genitals for small change

Vicious cycles that keep the Nigger and I AM

segregated

Living in a constant state of Niggerphobia

PORTRAIT OF THE POET AS A BLACK MAN

I've been called black, colored,

spook, jimmy, coon, eight ball,

jigaboo, jungle bunny, porch money,

sambo, shine, tar baby, negro,

spade, darkie, ape, and nigger

NIGGER

A man called me a Nigger who couldn't
pronounce my African name

Perhaps it was my unflinching gaze,
envisioning my ancestors in chains

Summoning crimes against humanity,
rape of African pubescent apparent
in my hue

Engulfed in constant denial and
condescending irreverence for greed
and contempt

I am cattle in his portfolio, stolen and sold
into slavery by African, European, and
American

Stripped naked of native tongue,
culture, family and homeland

When I am of no further use as a mule of
capitalism, they deny me an education and call
me ignorant

They deny me work and call me lazy

They inflict disease, arrest and
imprison black youths for fear of a
black planet

They call me boy, rapist, liar,
murderer, thief, to conceal their true
nature

Good for nothing, worthless, dull-
witted, dimwitted niggers go back to
Africa

To survive the African holocaust
we seek shelter in your shadows
to elude you

Cowardly, ignorant and docile servants
continue to work in the fields, as you
continue to rape the world, sip Mint Juleps
and dine on hors d'oeuvres

"I've never understood why the end of a relationship — especially one involving children — has to immediately signal a descent into hatred and toxicity."

— John Niven

SURVIVAL

Role of consummate victim is her found
philosophy
Psychosis the prognosis of post-traumatic
stress disorder
Unwilling actor in the character study of a
woman in rage

FALLEN FRUIT

Withering

No one's fault but her own

Damaged

Wayward journey into my strident company

CHOKING ON HER SLIT

Awoke, choking on her slit

Knowing I have to settle and

submit

ANATOMY

Condescending eyes, viral tongue
Inherent fear, passive and
deceptive nature
Anatomy burns like a diseased
whore

INNOCENCE WAS LOST

At thirteen, innocence was lost
Daddy's princess mirrors grown up
Mother turned tricks for rent
At thirteen, innocence was lost
Violation her weekly allowance
To forget she's only thirteen
All she ever wanted was love
Instead she contracts a disease
At thirteen innocence was lost
Guilt makes her repeat the sin
To forget she's only thirteen
Tormented and humiliated by incest
At thirteen, innocence was lost

ROT THAT TORMENTS

Unknowing child's pleas

Deafening words tear my fabric

In silence not to offend

Mother the rot that torments

At what cost betrayal of truth

A woman under the influence

Bottom feeding survivalist pretending

to be harmless

Far removed from this wretched

tribe that pollutes my seed

Sparing affliction of relation

to parasites and their wickedness

SURVIVALIST MANEUVERING IN PLAIN SIGHT

Infested with the necessity of
disappointment
Delusions lurk in the shadow of
forgetfulness
Nurtured by contempt and
misfortune
Masquerading as a TV mom until real
life interrupts the regularly scheduled
program

"Mistakes are part of being human. Appreciate your mistakes for what they are: precious life lessons that can only be learned the hard way. Unless it's a fatal mistake, which, at least, others can learn from."

— Al Franken

LEGACY

I want to be the father,

I never had

SCARS

Transactional repentance

Caducity skewed recollections

Photo albums distort claims

I remember everything

SENSITIVE SOUL OF MISFORTUNES

Devoid of trepidations I cannot

control

Plowing mother earth with erratic

impetus

In the name of God and Country, the

horrors

ADDICTION

Heightened perception of
oneness
Dosage barely nurtures
sickness
The more I pay, the more I'm
granted
Money the bond that seals my
fix
All roads inward lead to
despair
Surviving each day at war with
myself

ALLEGIANCE

I pledge allegiance to the flag
To murder your fathers and sons
Rape your mothers and daughters
Steal your land and resources
Spread disease, famine and disorder
With disdain and injustice for all

I'VE BEEN DYING FOR 43 YEARS, 17 HOURS AND 29 MINUTES

Survival's weary of my suicidal
tendencies
Dying for 43 years, 17 hours and 29
minutes
Company of evil men manipulating
the will of good men
Uncontrollable savages all knowing
of sacrificial lambs
Frequent stream of arrivals and
departures protruding like a fish
out of water

THE GREATER NOT THE LESSER

Descendant of slaves rooted in

detestation and exoneration

Piety of triviality belittles

true nature

Engulfed winds of battle, the

greater, not the lesser

Accomplices in the throw of

self-destruction

Indoctrinated philosophy of survival

of the fittest

Rebirth of a nation divided now

empathetic

Men overflowing with love, not

beasts impregnated with rage

DEAR GOD

I have given the Devil the pieces that
complete me
Self-medicating inner turmoil with substance
abuse
Invisible, running in circles tracking my own
shit
Solitary, regardless of sharing it with you
No desire to love and the only touch I need is
my own
I am the illegitimate Son of God and Man
Trapped in the Devil's womb waiting to inhale
Curtain falls on my nightly charade
No one will care that I am no longer
Lecherous and diabolical actor receiving
praise for staying in character
As THEY pretend to keep the sun out of their
eyes

UNDER THE GUISE OF DECEIT

Warred with the Devil

Lifeless, left for dead

Patient, resolute, steadfast

Demon revealed true intent

Under the guise of deceit

James Smith in front of Jean Michel Basquiat's and Andy Warhol's former studio on Great Jones Street NYC.